WORDS FROM THE HEART

a Compilation of Life Poems from a Survivor of Domestic Violence

WORDS FROM THE HEART

a Compilation of Life Poems from a Survivor of Domestic Violence

Dani Jones

HUNTER ENTERTAINMENT NETWORK
Colorado Springs, Colorado

Words from the Heart, a Compilation of Life Poems from a Survivor of Domestic Violence
Copyright ©2023 by Dani Jones
First Edition: October 2023

All rights reserved. No part of this book may be reproduced or transmitted in any form or by any means without written permission of the publisher, except in brief quotes or reviews. Unless otherwise noted, all Scripture is taken from the New King James Version of the Bible® (NKJV). Copyright © 1982 by Thomas Nelson. Used by permission.

To order products, or for any other correspondence:

Hunter Entertainment Network
Colorado Springs, Colorado 80840
www.hunter-ent-net.com
Tel. (253) 906-2160
E-mail: contact@hunter-entertainment.com
Or reach us on Facebook at: Hunter Entertainment Network
"Offering God's Heart to a Dying World"

This book and all other Hunter Entertainment Network™ Hunter Heart Publishing™, and Hunter Heart Kids™ books are available at Christian bookstores and distributors worldwide.

Chief Editor: Deborah G. Hunter
Book cover design: Phil Coles Independent Design
Layout & logos: Exousia Marketing Group www.exousiamg.com

ISBN: 9798865068327 (Paperback)

Printed in the United States of America.

Dedication

I want to dedicate this book to my children: Johnny, Isaiah, Amarissa, Jesse, Joshua, Elijah, Sarah, and Trinity, and also to my sister Tracy Jones, without whom I could not have made it this far in life. You guys are my rock!

Acknowledgments

I want to acknowledge my husband, Mike for standing by my side for all these years through thick and thin. He has helped me grow up and recover in so many ways from the abuse of my past, especially in those early days of our marriage. I love you, Mike!

I also want to acknowledge Maryruth Dilling, MSMHC, DTM for her supporting me as I wrote the bulk of these poems and worked on my recovery. She is my main supporter when it comes to my writing.

I also want to give a very special thanks to Natalie Hamm, LMFT for her dedication and hard work. She is an amazing therapist and is helping me over the large hurdles of trauma recovery. Natalie, I couldn't have done this without you!

Foreword

Maryruth Dilling, MSMHC, DTM

I met Dani shortly after the New Year in 2013. I started my internship at a local residential treatment facility. She was on my caseload. I knew Dani was different from the first time we met. I also knew that God had led me to be her particular counselor because of my own personal experiences.

As time passed and I learned more of her story, I was amazed at this woman's resiliency. I knew God had a special purpose for her life. Then, I began to see glimpses of her talent with the pen and the camera.

As part of Dani's healing journey, she created heartbreakingly beautiful poetry that expressed the pain of her experiences. Her poems also gave glimpses of the hope she still clung to. And her photos... amazing beauty in her micro-photography.

I began to encourage her to put the poems together with some pictures and make a book. I knew her story would help others who were also walking a similar journey. It's been ten years now. I cannot express the delight that I feel to know that she is finally taking that journey to share her story with others.

Some of the poems may be hard to read. They may trigger some unresolved issues for the reader. If this happens, I encourage the reader to find a trusted individual to share your own story with and seek God's help in healing.

God promises to give us beauty for ashes and the oil of joy for mourning (Isaiah 61:3). He is the Great Physician. He is the only one who can heal the wounds of the heart caused by those in our lives.

I pray that you will seek Him today. I pray that this journey through Dani's beautiful poetry will bring healing and the knowledge that there is someone who understands. I hope they make you cry, and make you laugh. Most of all, I hope you realize that God is there even when it doesn't feel like it.

God Bless,
Maryruth Dilling, MSMHC, DTM
Kindling Dreams

Foreword

Natalie Keese Hamm, LMFT

How many of us are living a life of authenticity? This book is a delightful journey inside the heart of the author. Danielle Jones has a poetic presentation that is raw and real, which touches the core soul of the reader.

Danielle's poems are representative of her life's struggles and triumphs. Her authentic poems are unique to her; however, her writing style is relatable to all of humanity. To be human is to have ups and downs and to experience vulnerability in one's life journey.

Danielle's writing is the unspoken voice of humanity. Danielle's book is a true invitation for all of us to gain insight into how our life experiences influence our inner world.

Table of Contents

Introduction 1

Chapter 1: Prayer 5

    My Life Prayer
    Prayer for the Morning
    The Vessel
    Your Praises
    In Jesus' Name

Chapter 2: Jesus 15

    Who am I
    All in Jesus' Name
    Jesus Carried Me
    Jesus is Waiting
    Name Above All Names
    The Commission

Chapter 3: Gratitude 25

    Free Indeed
    Where are You?
    Ashes to Beauty
    Forgiveness
    Safe
    Thank You
    Rise Up

Chapter 4: Friends & Family 41

    The Fristers
    Out with the Old
    My Trinity Rose

    My Princess Amarissa
    Man-Man
    Lead Me
    Johnny Boy
    Amanda
    A Volunteers Life at CWC
    A Single Rose
    My Angel on the Hill

Chapter 5: Deliverance 63

    Deliverance
    Fighting the Monster
    His Presence
    My Scars
    A Strange and Wonderful Way
    My Scarred Soul
    The Fight
    Why

Chapter 6: Comfort 81

    Peace, Joy & Hope
    Release
    Fear Not
    His Girl
    My Circle of Trees
    Proverbs 13:12 (ala Dani) my interpretation

Final Word from the Author 81

Meet the Author 97

Frail Old Angel

One night, I had the strangest dream… it left a tale to tell.
I dreamt I saw an angel… poor thing, she wasn't well.

Her body was bruised and battered… she looked so tired and worn.
I asked myself, "How could this be?" An angel so forlorn.

These bruises are from shielding you… in times of dire ill.
The destruction that's been done by you… I've often paid the bill.

My wings are ripped and torn… a noble badge I wear.
So many times, I've flown for you… from evils unaware.

Each scar has its own story… of deadly wounds destroyed.
You've made me wish (more times than not) that I was unemployed.

I only wish you could make it… standing on your own.
But my child, don't you worry now… you're never left alone.

For I'm here watching over you… until my powers fail.
Please try not to forget... I'm getting old and frail.

I could hardly believe my eyes… how much she must have cared.
I wept on her strong shoulders… and left her in despair.

When I woke in the morning, I thought "why should I try?"
Distantly, I thought I heard a frail angel cry.

                                                    Author Unknown

1
PRAYER

Chapter 1

PRAYER

MY LIFE PRAYER

Our Father who art in Heaven
Hallowed be Thy name
You saved my soul, You made me whole
I'll never be the same

Thank You for the life You gave
Your Son so pure, no sin
He died, His life upon the Cross
All so I could come in

Thy Kingdom come, Thy will be done
On Earth just as in Heaven
You gave me life and lots of love
And children number seven

There were eight from my womb that breathed on this Earth
All lovely and perfect and whole
But one You chose to take back home
Because You loved her soul

Give us this day our daily bread
Please Jesus, meet my needs
Forgive me for all I've done
The bad and selfish things

The things we do we know are bad
And the naughty callous thoughts
And the things we're not so sure
We do that hurt Your heart

Please guard my path, keep evil away
Help me to walk in Your will
Protect my heart and keep my mind
Your Spirit please infill

Lord, take my life and make it Yours
To walk how Jesus walked
To love the ones who hurt me most
The ones who always balked

Lord, let my life reflect Your love
Your mercy and Your grace
Please let Your joy live in my heart
And shine upon my face

Yours is the Kingdom, the power, the glory
Forever and ever and then
I thank You Lord for everything
In Jesus' name, AMEN

Dani Jones ©2013

PRAYER FOR THE MORNING

Good morning, Heavenly Father
I give to You this day
I thank You for the things I have
I'll let You have Your way

I want to be within Your will
And do as You would do
I give You every breath I have
And my emotions, too

Prayer

I thank You for my family
I thank You for Your love
I thank You for my trials
And Your mercy from above

I give to You my children
Thank You for Your grace
Thanks for the ability
To run the Christian race

Thank You, Lord, for what You've done
You made me new again
You healed my soul, made me whole
I'm able to see You again

To see the beauty in each day
And when the sky is grey
It's quite alright, I'll use that, too
To walk within Your ways

Please help me, to speak Your will
And walk within Your path
Keep on the straight and narrow road
Be thankful for what I have

Please help me to focus on only the good
And to pray for all the bad
To lift those up who hurt and cry
And what I don't understand

Thanks again for all You've done for filling me anew
I never dreamed I'd feel this way
It's all because of You

Thank You for my heart so new
And that I'm not the same
For everything I thank You Lord
Amen, in Jesus' name

Dani Jones ©2012

THE VESSEL

Noun—A craft for traveling on water, an airship, hollow or conclave utensil, a cup, pitcher, or vase. Used for holding liquids or other contents. A tube or duct as an artery, or vein, containing or conveying blood.

They are different shapes and different sizes. Some are tall and thin, and some are small and squat. Some are beautifully ornate, yet some cracked and chipped. All are made to carry something. A fluid of some sort; wine, water, milk, blood. God asks us to be His vessels to carry the Living Water to others, so they may have life and life more abundantly.

What do our vessels look like? Mine is kind of large where someone else's is smaller, but they are both meant to carry the same amount. Mine has a few cracks and chips. Jesus uses all our vessels as long as we are willing to let Him use them. (He's such a gentleman.)

Right now, Jesus is smoothing out the cracks and filling them in, so I can hold His Living Water.

As I go through this refining process (sanctification), God is blessing me and refining me and scraping off the dross. I believe He leaves the chips and seams, so He can show off our character.

Right now, I am carrying His blood along with His Living Water to others. Some will be filled by sharing the same cracks as me and others, I'll pour into them. But in the end, all will have and be their own vessels to share with others.

Dani Jones ©2013

YOUR PRAISES

Jesus, I love You
I praise You with my soul
You've always loved me
You've always made me whole

Praise starts in my heart
And comes out my mouth
It makes me dance
It makes me shout

Praise is a verb
Much more than a noun
My hands lifted up
My eyes looking down

My whole body moves
I won't make it stop
I dance with the wave
I dance with a hop

I sing to You praise
I give You my heart
I give You my everything
It's only the start

Praise for Your wonder
Praise for Your love
Praise for Your Spirit
From Heaven above

Praise for my safety
Praise for my life
Praise for forgiveness
For all of the strife

Praise for Your mercy
Praise for Your grace
Praise for Your victory
From that really hot place

My worship is due You
You've renewed my faith
You have protected me
From Hell's horrid fate

Sometimes, my praise is silent
Where there is no sound
My whole body sends praises
They're quiet, Heaven bound

Sometimes, I praise You loudly
And scream from the top of my lungs
I dance and drum and lift my hands
And sing to You my songs

But alas, in the end
It's all about You
'Cause to Jesus my Savior
All praises are due

Dani St. Onge ©2013

IN JESUS' NAME

Lord, why do I have to hurt so much
I'm tired of the fight
To keep my heart in just one piece
And make it stay upright

Why do people let us down
They don't do what they say
They always find a "better" friend
When they don't get their way

Prayer

There are different reasons to be used
It's over, it's me, it's God
Or business, sex, or not good times
Whatever, it's all odd

It seems to be easier to just pretend
That nothing rocks my boat
To be the strong resilient one
Not a lamb, but like a goat

To be hard and callous is the way
I used to live and act
I got by without the hurt
But lonely—it's a fact

I know that You want more for me
To be free from all the pain
My broken heart needs to be healed
I need to trust again

To see as You do from my heart
And yet not be so hurt
Or do I just go back in time
And figure I'm just dirt

I want to jump in Your arms
And blindly fall to You
And know that I will be alright
No matter what You do

I need direction from You, Lord
I don't know what to do
I want to walk within Your will
To stick to You like glue

And this time, I'm set aside
To grow, expand my walk
Not knowing what the next move is
I'm waiting for You to talk

Dani Jones

To tell me how to do my life
Which way to go is right
Just a word, or song, or endearing friend
To help shed some light

You say to love, but it always hurts
To put myself out there
To be soft and kind and open, too
When people just don't care

I'll try to walk within Your will
Be soft and kind, not hard
Please protect me, guide me there
My heart, oh Jesus, guard

I'll do Your will, give up my life
Answer Your call dear Lord
I know You'll get me where I need
With You Lord I'm not bored

I need direction, straight answers, God
So I can know which way
You want me to walk this out Lord
On You I'll call today

I'm sure You've heard my prayers dear Lord
'Cause Your ears are not deaf
I need my life encased in Yours
Or else it's sudden death

So, take my heart and all that's here
To do with as You please
You have control, You get to drive
I give You all my keys

Please help me Lord, to be so strong
And do Your will again
Thank You, Lord, for all You do
In Jesus' name, AMEN

Dani St. Onge ©2013

2
JESUS

Chapter 2

Jesus

WHO AM I

Your Word says that I'm Your child
I do not understand
How can that be when I feel wild
And do just what I can

You say I am complete in You
That You have made me whole
But how can that be Lord when
I feel I'm in a hole

Your Word tells me that You're my friend
You'll never leave my side
That I am complete in You
Because Your Son has died

His blood was shed so I might live
And become one with You
I've been redeemed, I've been set free
I want to feel that, too

Your Word says I'm significant
And that I'm salt and light
Lord, I want to shine for You
And help this world be bright

I am secure because You're there
You will not leave my side
I have no spirit of fear but power
Love and a sound mind

You came to save me with mercy and grace
You say my love for You
Makes you happy, makes You pleased
It doesn't make You blue

I am Your child, my future secure
And if You had a fridge
My picture and good work is there
Right beside the bridge

The way I came to know You, Lord
And talk to You in prayer
You take away all my sins
And peel back all the layers

Of sin that I have done in life
And ways that I have coped
Like lies and harm and so much more
You've done more than I hoped

You have adopted me, You've cleaned me up
And only shown me love
I thank You now for all You've done
My Savior from above

So now I know You've set me free
I'll never have to buy
That junk again from deep within
'Cause I know "Who am I"

Dani Jones ©2013

ALL IN JESUS' NAME

Betrayal and lies, some silver, a kiss
It all had to happen, there's nothing amiss
He suffered and died, so I might come in
To Heaven to live and be without sin

Like Jesus my Love, my Savior, my Light
He took all my sins that one fateful night
A life is now gone, I've been set free
That is what Jesus did just for me

He came to the Earth, so that I might live
On Calvary's Cross He took all my sin
My sins were so heavy, that burden to bare
He cried out to God who turned a deaf ear

He just couldn't look, from there on His throne
His Son had to die, my sins to atone
A borrowed tomb is where He lay
Behind that stone three nights and days

Then, on that day when Mary came
Life as we knew it would never be the same
Jesus was gone, raised up from the dead
The prophecy is done, like Scripture has said

He hung out in town for forty more days
His Spirit He'll leave us to light up our way
Pentecost happened the power of the Ghost
He gave us to guide us, our Heavenly Host

So that I may live and become Jesus' Bride
Forever in Heaven at Jesus' right side
He took all the heartache, the guilt, and the shame
All for my redemption, all in Jesus' name

Dani Jones ©2013

JESUS CARRIED ME

Jesus loves me this I know
He still loves me even though
I hurt His heart and made Him cry
He said to call, I didn't try

Repentance came to flood my soul
Grace and Mercy made me whole
I fell completely on His grace
I got before Him on my face

He picked me up and brushed me off
He didn't judge, He didn't scoff
He held me close in warm embrace
And wiped my tears from off my face

He whispered love into my ears
He took away all my fears
In Jesus, I have been redeemed
Freedom like I've never seen

The women He's placed into my life
Speak life, and love, and yet not strife
Lord, please help me I don't know how
To receive this love You give right now

Rejection and anger are the norm
A new me You have formed
You send acceptance, life, and love
It's all because of You above

Thank You, Lord, for Your breath
You've saved me from a certain death
I love You Lord and I won't stray
From the straight and narrow way

I'll keep You close; I'll hold You tight
Jesus, keep me in Your light
Please guard my path, so I don't stray
With You is where I want to stay

Thank You for Your love so sweet
Because my cares are at Your feet
I love You Lord cause You're the best
Cause You carried me through life's test

Dani Jones ©2013

JESUS IS WAITING

Mercy doesn't care what you've done
Grace is what atones
Mercy will carry you through
Grace is free for you
Jesus is waiting

Mercy helps you hold on
Grace is what atones
Mercy knocks on your heart
Grace sets you apart
Jesus is waiting

Mercy + Grace = Peace
Lay it all down at His feet
Mercy I grab
Grace I can have
Jesus is there

Thank You, Jesus, for Your love
For Mercy and Grace from up above
JESUS IS MINE!

Dani Jones ©2013

Dani Jones

NAME ABOVE ALL NAMES

Wonderful, Counselor, Prince of Peace, God
To me these words do not seem odd
Savior and Majesty, Redeemer and Lord
More than a proper noun, more than a verb

Deliverer, Protecter, the Great I AM
Jesus, The Mighty One, Comforter and
Jehovah Jireh—my provider, Yahweh Elohim
Lord of Lords, God Almighty, Shaddai, and El-Elam

Jehovah Rapha—The Lord who heals, Shalom is Lord our Peace
Yahweh means divine salvation, El-Roi is God who sees
Adonai was used for those who were not born a Jew
The Alpha Omega, Beginning and End,
and then there's Advocate, too

The Author of Eternal Salvation, the Author of our Faith
The Ancient of Days, the Author of Peace,
the One who came to save
The Bishop, The Branch, our Buckler, Our Bread,
The Bright and Morning Star
The Carpenter, the Chosen One, the Diadem of Beauty,
the All-Consuming Fire

Creator, Commander, Dayspring, and Door
The Dwelling Place Deliverer and oh so much more
Elect One, Emmanuel, Faithful and True
The Fortress, The Firstborn, The Cornerstone, too

Gentle Whisperer, Gift of God, the Glory of the Lord
All these names have references, they're all in His Word
God the Almighty, God over all, God of the whole Earth
High Priest, Great Shepherd, Hiding Place,
the head over All the Church

Jesus

Horn of salvation, my Husband,
my Hope, Jehovah, and Jesus, and Judge
Just One, Jealous One, and Intercessor, Jesus, and Christ, and God
My Keeper, my King, my Light, Messiah, and Mighty One
Merciful, Graceful, Offspring of David, the Only Begotten Son

The Physician, The Portion, The Potentate,
The Power and the Priest
Propitiation, the Purifier, He is the Prince of Peace
The Quickening, Refiner, Our Refuge, He Rules
Resurrection, Rewarder, The King of the Jews
Root of David, Rose of Sharon, Savior and Servant, and The Song
The Spirit, The Source, The Son of Man
The God above all Gods

Our Earthly minds can't comprehend
And so, we take a guess
We give Him all the coolest names
We give Him all the best

A name is more than just a word
It describes those that we love
Oh wait… because I forgot one
My Jesus is my Dove

Dani Jones ©2012

THE COMMISSION

Don't lie, don't steal
Love the Lord with zeal
Don't kill, love your momma
Give to God all the honor

Mercy and truth, humility, too
Kindness and love, all these things do
Be gentle, have faith
Be slow to anger, just wait

Husbands love your wives, wives love your man
Don't say you can't, with the Lord you can
Don't judge, find joy
Hold on tight, oh boy

Be chaste, no sex
Till married or be vexed
Forgive wrongs, acknowledge rights
Be still, He is the light

No idols, not one
Like a cow or the sun
Don't be lazy or just lay around
But dig in the dirt, till the ground

The Sabbath keep holy, on that day rest
Go to church and give God your best
Don't swear by Heaven alone
For it's our God's heavenly throne

Servants be good, your master you serve
Jesus will give you what you deserve
He's our God, Chose peace not wrath
Be still, be quiet

Dani Jones ©2011

3
GRATITUDE

Chapter 3

Gratitude

FREE INDEED

I need to be free
From destruction, guilt, and shame
I need to be free
To just be me
I need to be free
To be free, indeed

God tells me in His Word
That I am set free
He says I am His
That He loves me
In worship we sing praise
For freedom in Christ
We lift our hands, get on our knees
We're the apple of His eye

He died on the Cross
So, I could be free
He loves me so much
Why can't I see?
Worthless and empty
Is how I do feel
He says I am His
His blood is the seal

Redemption is nigh
For those found in Christ
He comforts His babes
The ones in the Light
I feel I'm alone
No comfort to find
I want to be whole
A babe in the Light

I know in my head
And some in my heart
There is freedom in those
In whose love He imparts
Jesus, I need You
Can't do this alone
My spirit's so dry
So dry as a bone

Your love and Your comfort
I'm longing to feel
To fill up my being
To completely heal
No more sadness
No big, dark, black hole
Please send me Your Spirit
In me please infill

I choose to be free
From destruction, guilt, and shame
I choose to be free
From isolation and self-gain
I choose to be free to just be me
I choose to be free
To be free, indeed

Dani Jones ©2013

WHERE ARE YOU?

Why can't I hear You?
Where are You now?
Why can't I feel You?
Have I broken my vow?

I try to hear You on the beach
Within the waves so deep
I try to hear You in the woods
In the rustle of the trees

Where have You gone? Why aren't You here?
I feel so all alone
In a multitude of people
I am the only one

I try to feel You in the wind
As it blows my hair awry
I try to feel You in the sun
But all I do is cry

The tears roll down my cheek so soft
I cannot seem to stop
They say You keep them in a jar
I wonder what's Your thought

Do You think that I'm a baby
For crying all the time
Or do You sit and wonder
If I'll ever call You mine?

And mean each word within my heart
And truly make You Lord
Or will I stop these foolish things
When eventually, I am bored?

I feel I've broken every vow
I've ever made to You
I think You're sitting on Your throne
Feeling oh so blue

I know it hurts Your heart to see
Me doing my own thing
I want to have integrity
Your praises I will sing

My heart, it has rebellion
I want it to be gone
I want to be excited
For the Great and Holy One

It seems to me to be so far
The future isn't bright
The hatred of myself is there
I know it isn't right

Jesus, please help me I want to feel
Your hands upon my heart
Help me to want to do Your will
To want to do my part

Thank You, Jesus, for loving me
And giving me Your Word
Please help me want to do Your ways
To fly free like a bird

"There is freedom in Christ" my friends all say
"There is joy within the walk"
But I am full of gloom and doom
Please Jesus, help me stop

I want to be a godly mom
A wife who knows the way
A woman who loves Jesus first
Someone who doesn't stray

Gratitude

But when rebellion stirs the pot
Self-loathing rears its head
I never run to Jesus first
I trust my gut, instead

I give You my heart, my mind, my will
Please help me walk in Your path
Give me strength to turn my head
And take a spiritual bath

To wash my mind, my heart, my will
To worship at Your feet
To put You first in everything
To feel Your own heartbeat

I give You now my everything
I'll give You all my best
And when my best is not enough
I'll give You all the rest

Dani Jones ©2013

ASHES TO BEAUTY

I'm the man on the street corner
Asking you for dimes
I'm the teen going to prison
For doing all those crimes

I'm the housewife who lives next door
Keeping my kids safe
From the monster that I married
Who hits me in the face

I'm that woman who walks the streets
I think love is found in men
I always walk the streets at night
I do the best I can

To make a dollar with my looks
I'm all dolled up this way
I think I've got them hooked tonight
Tomorrow's another day

I'm the guy in the business suit
The money's in the bank
I've got the booze, the drugs, the life
And just myself to thank

I'm the one who tends the bar
I'm happy all the time
At least you seem to think that's so
You cannot see inside

I'm the high society wife
Got clothes, the heels, the pool
I live the life; it seems so grand
My husband is the fool

One thing we have in common
We all have broken souls
We're empty, tired, we are lost
We're void, we have a hole

We look for things to fill it up
Like men and drugs and booze
Money and relationships
But all in all, we lose

Then, we hear of Jesus Christ
You say He is real cool
He can fill that hole today
And make us clean as wool

You say He wants to be our friend
To love us? Fill us up?
To wash our hearts and clean our minds?
We've only to look up?

Ask Him in to be our friend
To walk with Him today
To be our Lord our everything
And life will be okay?

Better and better, day by day
Just give Him all our stuff
He'll take all that we want to give
He wants more than just fluff

He's a gentlemen with those He loves
He doesn't push or shove or take
He wants to take our ashes
And throw them in the lake

He will make us beautiful
He'll clean us up inside
He'll take the ashes of our lives
Then smile at us with pride

He's cleaned us up, made us complete
And His Spirit makes us whole
He took our ashes all away
And made us beautiful

Dani Jones ©2013

FORGIVENESS

If somebody sins against you
The Word tells you what you should do
Go to them alone
Don't you dare moan
Get some help if that doesn't do

When Peter was asked to forgive
He said seven and then let them live
Seventy times seven
To get into Heaven
More than that, you don't count to forgive

To the servant the master advanced
Some shekels the servant had asked
Then, the master did say
To the servant to pay
Back the shekels the master advanced

The master forgave him the loan
To the servant he threw him a bone
Go home to your sons
And try to have fun
You are free and your sons won't be sold

Then, the servant he started to moan
Shekels to someone else he did loan
Give it to me
Or I'll murderize thee
Till the other man started to moan

Then, the master that deed he did hear
Someone else had tickled his ear
To the servant he made
To pay back what he paid
And now you will live in dark fear

So… forgiveness is what we must have
It's calming and somewhat like salve
To forgive brings you peace
Sometimes to your knees
And sometimes, it will make you laugh

Dani Jones ©2013

SAFE

Safe is when I'm in Your arms
When I'm feeling oh so blue
Safe is knowing You are there
And that You love me, too

Gratitude

To feel safe it is paramount
In order to move on
For me to grow and learn and be
To keep on keeping on

To walk the walk that Jesus did
All those years ago
To keep His standards all my days
To have the Spirit flow

I'm safe among those trusted friends
They're few and far between
The ones who love You, put You first
The ones who are not mean

To trust You Lord has been so hard
And though my heart does know
You're the One who kept me safe
All those years ago

I'm learning in You, I'm not so bad
That I can be O.K.
That in You, I'm a precious child
That Your love doesn't sway

That You protect me, keep me safe
You hold me in your palm
You nestle me beneath Your wing
It's You that keeps me calm

Jesus I love You, in You I will trust
To always keep me safe
I place in You my confidence
To show me of Your ways

I'm in a nest, a cocoon of sorts
I'm learning of Your will
To place my heart into Your hands
I'm learning to be still

Dani Jones

I came into this place a little worm
I'm tucking into You
I'm cleaning up my heart—Your home
I'm giving it to You

Please take my life, my mind, my will
I know You'll take good care
Of all those things that mean to me
My world, my heart, my air

So, safety it is paramount
For me to trust in You
To let You do all that You must
To make me like You, too

Thank You Lord for this safe place
The staff here and my friends
Because You're changing me to be
Like You Lord God and then

I'll be that one that You can trust
To do the job You want
Whatever You have one mind
I'll do it, I won't daunt

You keep me safe, You show me love
You hold me in Your hand
You think I'm precious, good, and kind
Though I don't understand

All I need to do is trust
And know You're in my heart
To let You guide me, show me how
Just let You do Your part

All in all, I know what's right
I'm going to put You first
I'll chew Your Word, praise Your name
I know You'll quench my thirst

So, thank You Jesus for that peace
That comes from having faith
For holding me close up to Your heart
And keeping me all safe

Dani Jones ©2013

THANK YOU

I'm thankful Lord for all You've done
You truly bless my soul
You gave me life, You gave me love
Within You, I am whole

There is so much You've given me
So much to thank You for
My children are Your blessings, Lord
Even when they make me sore

The air I breathe, the sun for warmth
The moon to shine in dark
The breeze to cool me in the heat
Trees to shade me in the park

There are mountains majesty
My favorite place to be
I fell in love, became one with You
You have completed me

The flowers You plant for me
Small and wild are
Some blessings You have given me
Today, You've raised the bar

God, I thank You for the little things
That most times I forget
Mercy streams in with the morning
With the grace the sun does set

Dani Jones

I'm thankful for creation and
The order You have made
You've taken care of every need
You even thought of shade

The little things like taste buds
So I can taste Your world
The cotton that grows in the fields
Just for my skirt that twirls

For color, Lord, You've blessed my eyes
You could do black and white
But You wanted me to see Your world
Not in darkness, but in light

Every creature has a purpose
You've included me in that
You made the bees for honey sweet
You even made the bat

And even though I don't know yet
My purpose in this life
You've assured me if I trust in You
You'll show me which way is right

So today, I want to thank You, Lord
For my little heart beats
For air to breathe and life to see
And for my taste buds by my teeth

Your awesomeness is all around
To taste and feel and see
Thank You, Lord for everything
But most for loving me

Dani Jones ©2013

RISE UP

In a raunchy little trailer
Cigarette stains on the walls
That's what my life consisted of
No going to the mall

The trailer was really little
Just 8 foot by 16
It was home to all nine of us
It didn't have a screen

The bathroom was unusable
The kids, they had no toys
We weren't a happy family
There really was no joy

I look back upon those years
Full of drugs and abuse
I wonder why I stayed with him
To be hated and abused

I thought I loved my babies so
Then why would I just stay
I thought that God would help me
Just make it go away

He did just that, but not for years
Those years we suffered so
He put a gun to his head
The trigger he let go

We were set free but didn't know
At least for the first year
And now that life is different
For him I shed no tears

Dani Jones

I won't let him hurt me
I won't let him win
But me and my babies
Will rise up again

Dani Jones ©2014

4
FRIENDS & FAMILY

Chapter 4

Friends & Family

THE FRISTERS

This little group of ragtag girls
Has become close to me
We're from all different walks of life
And Jesus is our key

We have shared our lives, bared our souls
Fileted our hearts, indeed
We're more than close, like sisters now
We've planted little seeds

Love and patience, smiles and tears
And knowing someone's junk
Has turned us into sister friends
We're FRISTERS—that's no bunk

I've never had a friend before
Who truly knew my heart
Has heard the bad stuff and doesn't judge
And will still hang out in the park

You guys don't think I'm mental
Sick, perverted, or worse
You all still love me no matter what
Even when I'm terse

Dani Jones

You are there to help me through
Those times I'm at my end
You'll talk me through, walk me through
Those times I need to bend

Sometimes, being flexible
Is not an easy task
We have all been there at times
We can't be afraid to ask

To call for prayer, an open heart
Or a shoulder for some tears
Maybe just a coffee date or a
Pair of listening ears

To hear our heart when times are tough
Or simply share a smile
I'm blessed to have you three for friends
Who will go that extra mile

I love you all and that's no joke
I know you love me, too
It's hard for me to comprehend
This friendship is like glue

Trina, you were there for me
That night I had to cut
You loved me through that confusing time
You didn't chew my butt

Denise, we have a different tie
We both each have a man
And even though we live apart
God's doing what He can

Our marriages are different yet
Almost just the same
I have to give control to God
Let Him take the reigns

Friends & Family

Anjelique, my frister, too
We live at UGM
The heart work we do at home
Is tough enough and then

We do a step study with our little group
Of ragtag fristers, too
But God, He helps clean out our hearts
Then, fixes them like new

The Holy Spirit is the glue
That holds us together
So we can go through all life's storms
And survive all of life's weather

Those ups and downs, those crazy nights
The happiness as well
Our dirty laundry has been aired
We swear we'll never tell

The Lord is good, He brought us here
For such a time as this
To be together, become close
My fristers, don't you miss

The blessing God has given us
This little motley crew
I have grown to love you girls
And yes, I even grew

Thank You Jesus for these girls
That You have given me
My eyes are open to their hearts
Thank You, I can see

We are blessed, we've been set free
Cause Jesus is the One
Who's banded us together here
To shine us out God's own Son

Fristers we are, fristers we'll be
As tight as grandma's gloves
And Jesus has us here right now
Growing us in His love

Dani Jones ©2013

OUT WITH THE OLD

There once was a girl named Dani
Who thought she was not worth a penny
She tried to walk tall
And sail through it all
But fell down upon her big fanny

She tried selling drugs in the city
Was widowed when her kids were just itty bitty
She met a new man
And thought that she can
Change her life even though it was gritty

She tried to call on the Savior
She asked Him to change her behavior
Change the bad into good
And give up the food

She started to change her behaviors
Things were still hard on this girl
Her hair was long and had a curl
She pulled some of it out
Without even a shout
So she cut off her hair with the curl

Then, God started working in her
Her flimsiness soon became sure
She shed that old life
With God there's no strife
And with Jesus, the girl became pure

Dani Jones ©2013

MY TRINITY ROSE

You are my baby
You always will be
You are my little
Mini-me

Your smile is so big
And your eyes light up
And someday you'll have
Your special pup

Your love of words
Is really cool
And you have gone
So far in school

A senior now
College next year
Photo and dance
That means lots of gear

You are growing up
Sometimes too fast
I want our friendship
To last and last

The older you get
The more you will see
The more you'll know
Your old mommy

I hope you'll look
At all of me
And please remember
All the times that we

Dani Jones

Sat together
Playing games
And talking over
Your children's names

I love you Beani
And that's the truth
Remember when we
Recovered the booth?

The picnics? The beaches?
And 4th of July's?
And drives where we're
Thinking of houses to buy?

The photoshoot
We planned out for you
Crazy make up
And silly hair dos?

My prayer for you
My youngest child
Is that you find God
And don't go wild

But finish school
Get your degree
Become that woman
You want to be

If you get side-swiped
And fall back down
Get on your feet
Don't you drown

You're smart and funny
And strong willed, too
God will show you
What to do

He'll keep you steady
And guide you, too
And really better
Than I can do

I'm just your mom
And I love you so
My little Beani
It's time to grow

This doesn't mean I like it
Or want it to be
But I need you to know
It's okay with me

Dani Jones ©2013

MY PRINCESS AMARISSA

Amarissa Danielle, my little princess
You were the first of my three girls
You were perfect, eyes of green
Your head had auburn curls

You were soft, delicate, and beautiful, too
I waited oh so long
For a daughter and ruffles and lace
So I could sing to you a song

Your brothers, they both loved you
But couldn't say your name
They were just two toddlers
So Sissy worked the same

But girl! You had a temper
From the first day that you were born
You held your breath, your face turned red
Your arms airborne

Dani Jones

You had mostly brothers growing up
And sisters numbered two
But you were so much older
So you showed them what to do

You were my little scrapper then
You didn't let me down
When your brothers picked on you
You didn't play around

You showed them who you thought was boss
You are still tough today
I know that you will be just fine
You keep those boys at bay

I am so sorry for the life
I chose that made you sad
For all those issues that you've faced
Including those from Dad

You grew up beautiful, pretty, and strong
Long hair and eyes so green
You may be tough but your heart is soft
Although it's rarely seen

You hide behind your gruffness dear
You don't let people in
But I know you cause you're my babe
I know just where you've been

I love you princess and I'm so proud
Of you and Peanut, too
She is your child, there is no doubt
She's got your temper, too

Now you've grown to womanhood
I hope we can be friends
I know our love will grow and grow
I hope it never ends

I want to be a friend to you
Way more than just your mom
Be safe and careful where you are
Please my dear, stay calm

Look to God to still your fears
He'll meet you where you are
Tuck into Him and read His Word
And He won't seem far

So my love, I give to you
These words here from my heart
You'll be home soon, so don't you fret
And God will do His part

Dani Jones ©2013

MAN-MAN

Eli, you were my smallest one
Who grew to be so tall
You were a sickly baby
Who couldn't breathe at all

Your asthma tried to kick your butt
You were sick your whole first year
You were in and out of hospitals
So sick you couldn't hear

I didn't know that you were deaf
Until you were age two
I noticed you had read my lips
So smart, my little you

You are funny, you laughed a lot
In your class at school
'Class clown' it was your name
The kids thought you were cool

Your personality is the bomb
You are the popular one
My youngest boy, my little man
The baby of my sons

Eli, you're a special babe
I can't tell you enough
Isaiah used to dress you up
And say that you were tough

Then, you grew up and made a choice
That wasn't very good
Now, you are in prison Hun
You didn't do what you should

Son, I love you this is true
Can't wait until you're home
I miss your face, I miss your hugs
But soon, the time will come

For us to spend time alone
We will go on a date
Texas Roadhouse is the place
For us to grab a steak

I'll see you soon, so please take care
Just keep yourself all safe
Prison is a real hard place
So pray and pray and pray

God is watching over you
My dearest, youngest man
Trust in God, lean into Him
I'll see you when I can

I'll pray for you, you pray for me
Just look to God, Eli
And so for now, I'm signing off
But it's not goodbye

Dani Jones ©2013

LEAD ME

Lead me with strength
Lead me with love
Lead me with passion
From God up above

Don't be bitter
Don't be hard
Please treat me fair
Don't be harsh

It's okay to be wrong
It keeps us humble
We aren't always right
That thought makes us stumble

Love Jesus the most
He won't lead you astray
Put Him before me
Every night, every day

Lead me with strength
Lead me with love
Lead me with passion
From God up above

Go to Him in prayer
Go to Him in song
If I fall asleep
Then, do it alone

Read what He says
Soak up every word
Cause a man full of God
Is the best in the world

He loves you my love
More than words can say
And I love you more
And more everyday

SO…
Lead me with strength
Lead me with love
Lead me with passion
From God up above

Dani Jones ©2013

JOHNNY BOY

Johnny, you're my first-born child
You are my number one
You were small, blond, so complete
My first little son

Your blue eyes twinkled when you smiled
You were a happy boy
You never crawled but only rolled
To grab some food or toy

As you grew so did your hair
Aunt Tracy cut your locks
You got scared, you tried to run
You cussed and then threw blocks

I'm sorry for your childhood
I could not keep you safe
I'm so sorry for the harm to you
I'm sorry for your fate

I love you son more than you know
I wish that you were here
I know that soon that time will come
Of that I do not fear

When you come home, we'll spend some time
We can go to the fair
And watch some movies at my house
And I will rub your hair

Until you're home son, I will pray
That you will search out God
Talk to Him, become His friend
And praying won't seem odd

Read your Bible every day
Every chance you get
Thank Him for your circumstance
It's not forever set

I love you Bud, so please take care
And keep my baby safe
You're all grown up now, guard your heart
Cause I can barely wait

For you to be here next to me
And cook a meal for you
I know you love me, so be safe
And you will be home soon

Dani Jones ©2013

AMANDA

Your smile is contagious
You always dress divine
Your heart is for Jesus
Your love for Him sublime

The girls here say they love you
You help us process thoughts
Your devo's very interesting
They take us on a jaunt

Dani Jones

Back in time, a life not known
History at its best
Your love for math is weird to me
Fractions?... Be my guest!

Amanda, you're special, you're one of a kind
You're sweet and docile, too
I love you sister for all those things
And you for being you

You have come to mean a lot to me
You tried to save my life
And in return, I was a jerk
By entertaining strife

Yet you forgive, you turn your cheek
Show mercy and some grace
You love me still and give me hugs
With that smile upon your face

I'm sorry I was such a brat
Your forgiveness, it is proof
That Jesus lives within your heart
With you He's not aloof

You're patient, kind, and funny, too
And you don't even judge
The girls who live within these walls
And you don't hold a grudge

Thank you again for who you are
Amanda, you're the bomb
You're the best, you passed the test
Of showing us God's love

Dani Jones ©04/22/2013

A VOLUNTEER'S LIFE AT CWC

You came from every walk of life
Just like the women here
Some with a past and some without
You all have become dear

A volunteer doesn't just give time
But your heart and wisdom, too
You can do more than just lead
You come beside us, too

You pray, you talk, you listen, too
You give your all to us
You help us to stay grounded
So we don't fight and fuss

But when tempers flare and voices rise
You help to keep us calm
You pray and point us to the Lord
So He gives Gilead's balm

Some are helpers in Voc-Ed
You help us to do math
Others get to check our rooms
And remind us to clean our baths

Some are in the admins chair
You handle all the calls
Without you to screen our guests
Some of us might fall

And some help in the kitchen, sweet
You help to chop and serve
Sometimes it's easy, sometimes it's tough
You're more than we deserve

Dani Jones

There are those who care for our kids
And play out in the shade
You're handy with a Kleenex, too
And the champ of all the Band-Aids

Some of you help keep us fit
And take us for a walk
Or help us with the recumbent bike
Even when we balk

Then, there are a special few
Who help us to look good
You fix our hair and give us style
Looking like a princess should

Some sort clothes and help us shop
Some teach us the Word
Some help keep the garden green
And some help keep the herd

We love you all, appreciate you, too
We want to lift you up
Enjoy your night, have lots of fun
And eat your fill of grub

I know that there are more of you
And I hope that you don't mind
If we give you all a big applause
And tell you that you're kind

Dani Jones ©09/12/2013

A SINGLE ROSE

A long stem rose
In the garden of life
Pink for the friendship
Your love and the light

Friends & Family

Green stem and some leaves
And a couple of thorns
Show the lessons in life
Grab the bull by the horns

The petals are feathers
And leaves fashioned so
They resemble the strength
Of flight to and fro

Yet so soft and delicate
And gentle and kind
My friendship with you
Is what comes to mind

You are blessed among women
Of that there's no doubt
You lead by example
Speak softly, don't shout

Your trust is in Jesus
He carries you through
You tell other women
"It's Jesus, not you"

God's garden is big
You are one little rose
He loves you and prunes you
He helps you to grow

You're funny and clever
And spunky and fun
Your locks long and curly
Are tucked up in a bun

"It's not about me"
You selflessly say
"It's about my Redeemer"
"He's Jesus—The Way"

Your family is special
And most dear to you
You teach them of God
And all He can do

The others are there
You usher them down
Life's road—"Do be careful
On the bumps—don't you frown"

"Trust Jesus my friend"
You say with a smile
You always choose peace
Go the extra mile

God uses you Cindy
To help us all through
Life's ups and downs
And we all love you

A single rose
In the garden of life
You have blessed us all
With your love of God's Light

Dani Jones ©03/22/2011

MY ANGEL ON THE HILL

So pure and sweet and delicate
Lovely and beautiful, too
You're precious and special and one of a kind
And missed an awful lot, too

So short your time on this Earth
But special all the same
God needed you to come back home
And so, He called your name

Friends & Family

I love you so much, sometimes it hurts
To think that you're not here
For me to love, for me to hold
And wipe away your tears

Alas that job was not for me
And though it makes me sad
I know you're safe in Father's arms
No sadness you have had

Sarah, I love you and miss you so much
But I'm glad you are home
I know someday I'll see you soon
I know you're not alone

You left this Earth to be with God
Your presence He did want
No sickness, no heartache, no bump on the knee
Bad dreams they cannot haunt

God showed you mercy when He took you home
Gold streets where you live with
No shame, no sin, no poverty
Just grace and mercy... WOW

Sarah, I love you and I want you to know
I would have done my best
To give you love and happiness
But Jesus does that best

But you know this, that I am sure
There is nothing I can say
That you don't know or feel or see
I'll let God have His way

And though it's hard and makes me cry
I know it's for the best
In God's arms is solitude
And peaceful, loving rest

So, in the end I want to say
To God who holds you still
Thank You for my time with her
My angel on the hill

Dani Jones ©10/24/2012

5
DELIVERANCE

Chapter 5

Deliverance

DELIVERANCE

Deliverance—
A breath of fresh air, God touching my soul
His love and mercy and truth
From drinking and drugs and hurtful things
And things I've done since youth
A dance, some tears, a cleaning out
Of all the yucky stuff
His grace, His time, His perfect peace
The glory of His love

Deliverance—
It's wild, it's crazy, it's absolute
In a gentle kind of way
It's strange, it's wonderful, it's unique
When I let God have His way
Scary and lovely and oh so good
When Jesus touches you
Forget what others have to say
You know what you must do

Deliverance—
Be thankful and grateful and let it just come
Be still and soak it all in
Let Jesus control your heart and mind
Let Him remove the sin
Let Him fill you up with good
Let Him rule your life
Let Him suffer all for you
Let Him take all the strife
It's scripture, it's blood, it's atonement for sin
It's comfort at its best
It's Jesus doing what He wills
It's putting sin to rest

Deliverance—

Dani Jones ©2013

FIGHTING THE MONSTER

What is the monster
That threatens my life
What is the darkness
That whispers those lies

The ones that I hear
From the deep, dark, far past
They won't go away
They just laugh and laugh

They tell me I'm worthless
And stupid and dumb
I should go sit in a corner
And just suck my thumb

Why does it bother me
And haunt me so much
Why do the dreams come
They scare me so much

Deliverance

I cry out to God
His mercy He blew
Be still my small child
I'll carry you through

Don't be afraid now
This monster won't bite
Just cry out to Me
And I'll turn on My Light

The evil can't stay
Where do I reside
So come to Me child
Come to My side

In order for evil
To completely fade away
You need to forgive him
Stay close to Me, don't sway

Just walk on the water
Stand firm in your faith
Stay with Me in the bottom
Of the boat—you'll be safe

I'm sorry Lord for how I feel
I cannot seem to change
Part of me hopes that he's in Hell
On fire with balls and chains

Another part that's smaller still
Does hope he passed the gate
That's made of pearl at Heavens door
I hope he wasn't late

Please help me Lord, just to be still
And wait upon Your voice
Your love and peace and happiness
On You I've made my choice

So, help me trust, rely on You
To make that monster leave
To face it like a giant wave
On You I must believe

Help me God to love that man
And see him as You do
Forgive the pain, abuse, and hurt
The hell he put me through

I can't do this all on my own
On You I must rely
Cause if I don't, he'll eat me up
And I will surely die

Thank You Lord for steadfast love
Your mercy and Your grace
You hold my hand while I do walk
You even showed him grace

He had some seconds to call on You
Go boldly to Your throne
To say he's sorry and repent
And so, You threw a bone

But this story is 'bout me
And the fear to face the pain
To forgive him and trust in You
That it won't happen again

And so, I'll stand behind You, Lord
And trust that You will dig
Out all the hate and bitterness
So then, he's not so big

Dani Jones ©2013

HIS PRESENCE

Lord, I know You know my heart
My desires and my sin
I know Your love is very deep
Oh please let me come in

Your presence is perfect, lovely, and deep
Envelope me in You please
It's pure and whole and warm and calm
I melt in You with ease

Sometimes, I don't feel worthy
To bask within Your love
I feel like dirt, I am no good
Yet You smile on me from above

You look on me with loving eyes
A smile upon Your face
I'm Your delight, You boast on me
From Your throne up above

And though I do not understand
How You can love me so
With all my sin and prideful self
My heart, Lord, You do know

You know how much I want to serve
To be within Your will
You also know my sinfulness
And yet You love me still

And so right now it's hard for me
To feel You in my life
I see the blessings You bestow
Upon me as your Bride

I know in time I will be filled
Of only Your good peace
And so I'll wait and try to do
Your will and Word I eat

I need to feast, and chew, and chomp
Devour it all up
And read some more, soak You all in
And then Lord, we will sup

Together, we will make it through
The trouble and the trials
Thank You Lord for loving me
And holding me all the while

Dani Jones ©2013

MY SCARS

My scars aren't pretty
But they're part of me
I didn't get them from a fall
Or climbing up a tree

I got them from my choices
In how I handled strife
With razor blades and lighters hot
The way I lived through life

I know He cares for little me
My brokenness to use
To grow me up and give me strength
My stubbornness to lose

I used to choose to numb on out
By cutting up my skin
Or burning it or breaking it
Whatever mood I'm in

But now, I've learned to go to God
For healing and for help
And in return, He comforts me
Not put me on a shelf

He uses my past to help me now
And I keep my choices clean
When I am in much anguished pain
No more being mean

Not to myself in anyway
Just give it all to Him
And He will heal and change my life
My chances are more than slim

This little note is just some words
And a simple little rhyme
To let you know I turn to Him
He heals me in His time

If just one human grows from me
And from this story true
Then all is well in Jesus' name
And He can heal you, too

Dani Jones ©03/17/2018

A STRANGE AND WONDERFUL WAY

It's amazing what the Lord can do
When you pray to Him each day
He's there for you, He's got your back
In a strange and wonderful way

He answers back, He's by your side
He watches over you
He makes us all well, He heals your heart
He even heals mine, too

He loves us so He tells us true
His Book it lights the way
In Psalms, He guards your mind and soul
In a strange and wonderful way

In Acts, He is powerful, lovely, yet true
In Job, He turns a blind eye
But then in the end, He's always right there
Because He loves you and I

In Proverbs, He does give us clues
Of how to act each day
He is right there right in my heart
In a strange and wonderful way

In Revelation, He's coming again
Upon a white horse He will ride
He'll seek me out because I am His
I won't have to run or hide

Jesus, He's true and He's just and He's kind
And upon a cross He did lay
All at once to keep me His
In a strange and wonderful way

I'm thankful for the love of God
His words to me are true
Again, I'm thankful for His Light
And the way He loves me and you

All in all, He's right for me
I'm glad He's here today
He saved my soul, He's made me whole
In a strange and wonderful way

Dani Jones ©08/27/2018

MY SCARRED SOUL

My scarred soul cries aloud to God
For healing, love, and life
It has been broken and torn down
From battles, tears, and strife

The life I've led, the heavy fights
Have been tumultuous
There're lots of fears and ups and downs
It hasn't been harmonious

I've struggled with so much in life
Like money, booze, and drugs
Almost all of my short life
I've swept under the rug

If it's not there, it's way down deep
It can't exist for me
I can pretend that it is gone
And I'm okay, you see

When I was a little girl
Playing with my friend
My sweet and my young innocence
Was coming to an end

Her sisters taught me about a life
That was not meant for me
But a life that was for grown-ups then
And somewhere, I lost me

I was just a little girl back then
Who didn't know how to cope
They helped me out, they gave to me
Some booze, some smokes, some dope

I grew up a kid with different beliefs
Than most children of my age
I blamed myself for all things wrong
Even those I couldn't gauge

Life was hard and the years passed by
And sixteen was the age
I moved out, I got a job
Life turned another page

Two lives I led, one good and one bad
Parties were the norm
Church and pray on Sunday and
The week was safe from harm

How I couldn't have been more wrong
I'm sure it hurt God's heart
To do my thing, ignore His Son
And play with fiery darts

Then, to the chapel I do go
Prince Charming on my arm
It didn't take long for him
To lose his cunning charm

The fights were bad, the drugs were hard
What happened to my man
I prayed, and prayed, and prayed to God
Please save me if You can

But nothing happened, or so I thought
The Lord had left my side
The only thing that I could do
I thought, was run, and hide

I hid from God, I turned to me
No mercy was in sight
The drugs got harder, the smoke intense
I cowered down in fright

Deliverance

Then, one day a fight pursued
The mother and her son
They argued quite intensively
Then, he pulled out a gun

He was angry, the wife was scared
The children sat and cried
He yelled some more, the trigger pulled
The son fell down and died

Now, I'm safe but all alone
Eight children I now have
I call on friends who point to God
He'll heal you with His salve

Then, there came another man
He's different from the first
He promises to love and hold
And help quench my thirst

The children now they number twelve
With one in heaven above
We all live together in a ramshackle house
We try to live on love

The kids are mad, they don't understand
Why we had to marry
They were young, we were naive
It was too much to carry

All through this time, I try to smile
And fake that life's okay
I'm broken, hurt, I'm scared and torn
I still don't know the way

The kids grew up and moved away
They left us all alone
We only have each other's lies
And falseness to atone

Then, I learned that God is love
Relational is He
And even though I hurt His heart
He still wants little me

The little girl still lives with fear
She doesn't trust Him yet
But soon enough, He shows her life
Salvation she has met

The couple choose to live apart
And seek the Lord full on
They worship, they praise, they're finding their life
No more Satan's spawn

God doesn't promise roses or an easy life for me
I'm just a chunk of coal
With mercy and grace, He promises me
To heal my scarred-up soul

Dani Jones ©2013

THE FIGHT

I fight for safety
I fight for love
I fight for freedom
From fleshy gloves

I fight for purity
I fight for life
I am so tired
Of all the strife

Why do I feel
I can't measure up
That I'm not worthy
Of Your love

Deliverance

To share my heart
Is just too much
To do right now
To open up

I don't know how
To receive the good
That You send forth
I know I should

I self-sabotage
I ruin those things
The things that You give
That Your love brings

I don't feel worthy
Your grace to receive
It's hard to walk through
I fight not to leave

To run to the hills
To drive really fast
To get far away
From my horrible past

My emotions are crazy
I just want to be done
Please show me the way Lord
You are the one

Who holds the answers
Of how I should walk
I give You the key now
The one to my heart

Please take me and mold me
The way that You want
The fight is over
My Jesus, You've won

Dani Jones ©2013

WHY

Why are children made to suffer
Life's callousness and rains
Why did I have the life I've had
My childhood with its pains

I don't understand what you see
In my little finite mind
Why have people hurt me bad
And for years, I didn't find

The reason that lies inside my heart
The hurt that becomes tears
Why I had to hurt myself
Why I'm full of fear

The anger I have hidden inside
My emotions can't contain
The sadness, the hate, the bitterness
Where nothing good remains

I wonder where You were that day
Those "women" grew me up
I felt so dirty, bad, and worse
I drank from Judas' cup

That was just the first of many
Times I've let You down
Why do these things happen, Lord
I may as well go drown

Please forgive me of this sin
Please take it all away
Please help me to have some strength
I do not want to sway

Deliverance

Flawed and empty I come to You
So, I don't face Judas' end
I need relief, I need Your love
On You I must depend

This world it will not help me
And so, I come to You
To clean my heart, renew my mind
Restore my joy, please, too

I am so sad I can't forgive
That evil done to me
I need Your help, I need Your grace
I need to be set free

This burden is heavy and oh so hard
Too much for me to bear
I want to kick, and scream, and yell so loud
I need You God to hear

My heart is broken beyond repair
I'm down upon my knees
Please Jesus, please draw near
Please listen to my pleas

You're all I have, I come to You
God help me to forgive
Cleanse my soul and make me whole
All so that I can live

Why God do I wait so long
To call upon Your name
The longer it takes, the harder it gets
And things remain the same

Dani Jones ©2013

6
COMFORT

Chapter 6

Comfort

PEACE, JOY, AND HOPE

Why do some things seem evasive
Allusive, far away
They're things that aren't for me
At least not for today

The cool stuff, the good stuff
The right stuff from God
Like peace, joy, and happiness
To me those things seem odd

They're foreign and scary
Nowhere to be found
I can't seem to keep them
I'm always so down

A friend says elusive
Like fairies that fly
They come for a minute
Then, take to the sky

Why am I always waiting
For these good things to come
I have them for a day
And then, they are gone

Dani Jones

I'm told that I sabotage
The good things in life
I'm comfy with chaos
Destruction and strife

I've mostly experienced
The bad stuff—oh boy
Not so much happiness
Peace, hope, and joy

The Bible does tell me
To wait upon God
My faith does not waiver
My trusting is flawed

Hope equals fear
Depression and more
I wait for that rug
To come off the floor

Then, I fall to my knees
With tears on my face
Maybe, I'm not good enough
To run in the race

The race that Your Word says
To endure to the end
I'm broken and I'm down
I'm way far past bend

I only want integrity
Hope, joy, and love
That peace that surpasses
That comes from above

It seems foreign to me
And I don't quite know why
Jesus, please hear me
Attend to my cry

Comfort

I'm thankful for the things
You've placed in my path
I know I will gain them
If only I grasp

Those good times You fill me
With the things that are right
They shouldn't scare me
I'll just hold on tight

I know You will comfort me
And calm all my fears
Jesus, please help me
And wipe all my tears

Help me to trust You
You have never lied
Your Spirit is in me
That's why You have died

To hope for tomorrow
For peace from this war
That rages inside me
I can't reach that door

The one in my heart, God
Where You patiently knock
But I've barred all the windows
The doors, they're all locked

Why is it hard now
To feel that calm peace
My old man is begging
It cries for release

I'm wrapped up in chains
And I can't find the key
I don't want to sabotage
What You have for me

Dani Jones

Please let those fairies
Of hope, joy, and peace
Light on my spirit
And give me release

"It's time to start work child"
You lovingly say
"Ok" is what I answer
Please have Your way

I'll try to be still
While You work on my heart
I want to be steady
And not fall apart

To walk through this door
And integrity, too
I'll loosen the chains and
Unlock those doors, too

Please come and fill me
Please show me to hope
I invite You inside Lord
I won't tell you nope

I know You are there Lord
And sometimes it's hard
To clean up my own house
The garage and the yard

It's easy to help those
And not look at me
Cause then they're important
I don't have to see

My own junk and garbage
I need to clean up
But I must tend to it
So with You I can sup

I'll do it, I'll take it
And give it to You
And You will still love me
And make me brand new

Dani Jones ©07/04/2013

RELEASE

We all need release at times
It's part of who we are
Sometimes, I even find it
When I'm driving in my car

The faster, the better
Be careful when you stop
Do it on a country road
Just avoid the cops

Sometimes, we find release while
We are shopping at a store
And then the money is always spent
Before we hit the door

We buy for this one, get for him
Remember where you're at
Billy-Bob could use some shoes
And Susie wants a hat

Taking your friends out for a treat
A gooey hits the spot
Then the movies and dinner, too
Sometimes, it's hard to stop

Release can be found out at the gym
That treadmill is your friend
The elliptical is a new hot thing
The recumbent bikes the trend

Dani Jones

Some people find their niche in sex
And they don't care with whom
As long as there is some release
They feel they won't be blue

Depression and anxiety
Are friends of mine you see
They buddy up—make tension rise
They need release from me

I pull my hair or scratch my skin
Pop my knuckles out of joint
I need release, it's prevalent
I don't care at this point

Release has been my enemy
It quickly goes away
I need some help, I don't know how
Make it, please, just stay

God's created a release for you
My sisters tell me truth
It's all right here, it's in His Word
You don't have to be a sleuth

It's pretty simple, please just try
Ask Jesus in your heart
He will help you, keep you calm
He'll even do His part

With me, it is photography
And writing me out some prose
I write about experience
And photograph a rose

God talks to me in photographs
His Word it does ring true
I'm sorry if I seem amiss
It really isn't you

Comfort

I battle for release you see
It does torment my head
Sometimes, the feeling was so strong
I wished that I were dead

But Jesus came to heal my head
And give me His release
I've only just to give my all
My Lord I am to please

So, in the end, I just don't need
The gym, the food, the sex
The cars, the money, or some shoes
Those things just get me vexed

I'll try to put my trust in God
Believe that He will do
All of those things His Word does say
And stick to me like glue

Release is not a feeling
But it is a state of mind
It is a treasured lesson
One I'm hoping I will find

By running first to Jesus
And then calling on a friend
Release can be within His will
I hope this doesn't end

I love You Lord with all my heart
I'll call upon Your name
You'll keep me safe inside these walls
I'll never be the same

Thank You Lord for Your release
For helping me stay calm
For showing me my life is good
Protected me in Your palm

Dani Jones ©06/18/2013

FEAR NOT

You tell me not to be afraid
You say to trust in You
You tell me You'll give peace to me
And quiet my insides, too

You created the wilderness
The thunder and the rain
The lightening and darkness, too
They should not cause me pain

When I'm afraid, it's hard to call
On You I must depend
Cause You created everything
And Your love never ends

Jesus, please, I need Your help
Please answer my cry
I'll be strong, I'll trust in You
At least Lord, I will try

The thunder it does scare me so
The girls say that You talk
It's God that speaks, just trust in Him
Oh Dani, take a walk

Face your fears, you'll be okay
God will calm your heart
Pray for comfort and for peace
And Jesus won't depart

I'll trust in You Lord, I'll try real hard
To let You calm my soul
To take that walk, rely on You
Calmness is my goal

Thank You Jesus for Your peace
And all that You've given me
The tunnel is dark and there's a light
That I can plainly see

Comfort

So, I'll keep on praying, trust in You
Because You are the One
Who gives me peace and takes away
The rain and gives me sun

Dani Jones ©06/30/2013

HIS GIRL

To Him, I am beautiful
I'm lovely, I shine
His favorite, His special one
His one of a kind

To Him I am gorgeous
As soft as a lamb
He loves me with dimples
And just as I am

I'm His girl—
He tells me in Scripture so true
He desires me, He loves me
I desire Him, too

In Psalms, He's my Lord
My Savior, my Love
In Isaiah, my Husband
Revelation, my Dove

In Proverbs, my Rescue
My wisdom, my King
My Father, my Protector
He's my Everything

In Job, my Protection
In Psalm, a Strong Tower
In Matthew, Forgiveness
Acts brings us Power

He says I'm His favorite
His one of kind
A greater love than this
I'll never find

I am His Bride
All dressed up in white
He's patient, He's gentle
Yet willing to fight

He'll fight for my soul
His anger unfurled
He'll beat up the devil
Cause I am His Girl

Dani Jones ©2013

MY CIRCLE OF TREES

My circle of trees
Are tall and green
They watch over me
So, I'm not seen

They protect me, they shade me
They pray with me, too
They reach way high up in the sky
When it's pretty and so blue

The wind makes them bend
Back and forth, to and fro
The leaves wiggle around
When the wind starts to blow

They look like they're dancing
In a ballroom so big
The sky is the limit
The boughs like a lid

Comfort

My circle of trees
Their branches are strong
They hold up my swing
When I'm singing a song

They're tall and majestic
And beautifully toned
Their colors are gorgeous
They're perfectly honed

We thank God together
For Creation divine
Together we praise Him
His love is sublime

God gave me these things
My circle of trees
Their bark keeps them strong
And one has bees

I hung up a hammock
Secured it with a rope
I talk there with God
And He gives me hope

That's one thing I've asked for
That He gave to me
I share with my Beloved
Little circle of trees

Dani Jones ©06/29/2013

PROVERBS 13:12 (A LA DANI) my interpretation

Hope—what is this elusive thing
What does it mean for me?
Where is it found in life?
I cannot plainly see

Dani Jones

To hope is to expect, be still
But what per say is that?
Expect the good things? Wait on God
Is that where it's at?

It's something that doesn't come
To me without regret
The Bible says to wait it out
And so, I sit and sit

I expect good but am let down
And end up sobbing tears
I wait and hope for life to change
To be void of all my fears

God He does so much for me
And I still fight the good
I tear it down; I break it up
Just as if it's wood

I'd chop in pieces for my heat
To warm my broken soul
To make a little wooden cart
I end up in a hole

To hope is to be let down again
I cannot stand the pain
Of wishing, hoping, looking out
For a peaceful heart again

To rely and leave control to God
I cannot seem to do
"Trust Me child, be still just wait
I know what's best for you"

I feel the need to know which way
The Lord would have me turn
My insides doing summersaults
Just like a butter churn

Comfort

But since I don't know which way to go
I have to sit and wait
"Be still and KNOW that I am God
Cause child, I'm NEVER late"

He runs His time not by the moon
Or when the sun does set
But He always seems to do what's best
On that one I can bet

To hope is to expect, which means
To sit, I must be still
And wait on God to do His thing
His peace to me infill

So, I will sit and try to wait
For God to answer me
Because He's God and I am not
But that is plain to see

Thank You for Your Scripture God
For that hope deferred
Because when the time does come
I'll fly free like a bird

When desire comes, it will be life
Calming my broken heart
A tree of life the Word does say
To be still, it is my part

God does work in mysterious ways
Surprises round every bend
It will come if I just hope
His peace it will descend

Upon my heart because I've hoped
And waited and was still
God will come to me and say
"Peace My child, be filled"

Dani Jones

So thank You, Lord for the chance to wait
Be still and trust my life
To You today and then expect
And hope You'll take the strife

That seems to rule within my soul
That battles for the good
I'll be still and wait on You
And put away that wood

Dani Jones ©2013

Final Word from the Author

Hi there! First, I want to thank you for taking that first step of faith by purchasing this book. It is all Jesus. He helped me to write these poems. Some were written out of pure happiness, some from a place of total despair. Some were written to people and some about people, and some were about my life as I led it. All in all, I just want to give my praise and honor and thanks to Jesus for helping me throughout all those times in my life and giving me the words and strength to get through those years. I am a stronger woman because of the life I have been through.

I lived through many years of severe domestic abuse with nowhere to run to (in those days, they didn't have places and people to help like they do now). I had eight babies and God carried us all through the fire to the other side. Sarah is in Heaven with Jesus and the rest of my children are strong and living life. This book is our history and I pray you have enjoyed it.

If you or someone you know is suffering with domestic violence, call the National Domestic Violence Hotline at 1-800-799- SAFE.

Meet the Author

Dani Jones is a woman rising like the phoenix from the ashes. A resident of North Idaho, Dani is a mother of eight and stepmother to five. She has twenty-five beautiful grandbabies and one great granddaughter, she is extremely happy with.

Dani has survived more than thirteen years of severe spousal abuse of which she has come out on top.

Printed in Dunstable, United Kingdom